Leadership Development in You&#95;&#95;&#95;&#95;&#95;&#95;&#95;&#95; Developing
a simple system for developing leaders

Dr. William Clark

Printed in the United States of America

First Printing, 2016


Willis Dawson Publishing House

PO Box 193

Windsor, CT 06095

# Table of Contents

# Introduction

Leading a church is one of the biggest challenges anyone can take on. The leadership of a church is tied to several recognizable positions, and these include the roles of apostles, prophets, evangelists, pastors, teachers, and deacons. Most churches are structured with the simplest and common organizational structure that includes leaders in the role of pastor, deacon, and ministry leaders. Even with this simple structure, church leaders struggle to lead their followers effectively. Leadership development within the context of a local church should not include a blanketed approach. Blanketed approaches to leadership do not take into account the nuances of the local church's politics, membership demography, and leadership composition.

Therefore, this book seeks to provide pastors a way to bridge the gap between an "ideal leadership state" and the current state of leadership within their church. That bridge includes understanding the basics of leadership development, measuring the quality of a leadership development system, and coaching up emerging leaders.

## Leadership Basics

Leadership is the process of influencing others to achieve a goal. The effectiveness of a leader's ability to influence a group of people is based on that leader's capacity to provide synergy around a specific direction. The goodwill that is developed by a leaders' influence is strengthened by their ability to compel followers to action. How is this done? The leader must be aware of the needs of the followers, understand the things that cause reactions from followers, and have relatable experiences followers can trust in.

Defining leadership as a process suggests that leaders are not born, but they are made. Leaders use influence as a standard practice to guide their interactions with followers. This does not mean that leadership is an emotionless exchange between a leader and his followers; rather, the leader is aware of the inner workings of followers and knows how to encourage performance that can yield meaningful results.

The influence of a leader is maximized as they align the goals of individuals with the goals of the organization. For the sake of the organization, it is important for these goals to align because the organization can trust that followers will commit their energy to meeting the goals that matter to them. As a consequence, the organization has their goals met without having to provide additional motivation and incentive to sustain or improve individual performance.

Developing leaders requires some sense of a system that organizes the development of everyone that enters the program. As the team rallies around a common goal, a leadership development system can be developed; with the purpose of helping as many team members as possible, to utilize their current set of skills to take on a leadership role. A leadership role does not have to be defined by the title a person takes on; rather, the leadership of a person is defined by their willingness to take on new responsibilities.

## Leader Development through Coaching

Strong leadership development must include coaching. Coaching helps emerging leaders work on underdeveloped areas of their leadership, confront the challenges that are limiting their growth, and establish accountability toward reaching and sustaining success. Great coaching provides valuable support and objective guidance to the coachee because of a holistic perspective of a broader landscape. This view improves the effectiveness of a leader and ultimately helps the organization and team under their leadership.

A strong relationship between a coach and coachee is similar to the path-goal theory of leadership. This theory espouses that, the leader helps followers along their journey to meet their individual goals, by projecting specific leadership behaviors that fit the coaching need. The coach has the option to exhibit directive, supportive, participative, or achievement tactics based on the progress the coachee is making.

- Directive leadership gives instructions. The coachee relies on these directions because of the need for instruction, or because the demands of current circumstances warrant a top-down instructional approach to solving a problem.

- Supportive leaders are approachable and attend to the well-being and human needs of followers. The coach employs the individual consideration method of transformational leadership to ensure individual success based on a coaching plan tailored for the coachee.

- Participative leaders invite subordinates to share in decision-making. The coach introduces a macro view to the coachee, while the coachee introduces a micro view of the same situation.

A collaborative approach to solving a problem is developed, and that includes both perspectives.

- Achievement-oriented leadership challenges followers to perform their work at the highest level possible. The coach presents assignments to the coachee to expand their capabilities beyond their current limitations. The performance of the coachee systematically improves and creates new limitations.

Within the church, coaching is a viable leadership development method. Through coaching, pastors will see:

(1) An increase in the number of activities, which emerging leaders take responsibility for,

(2) An increase in the ownership, which emerging leaders take in as the tasks they are responsible for or involved in,

(3) An increased or renewed interest in being a leader, and

(4) A desire for leadership development.

The reason for these changes are because good coaches do not attempt to be the person they are coaching or attempt to live (or lead) vicariously through the coachee.

As pastors grapple with the development of leaders, coaching serves as a reminder that (1) when someone thinks they know something, they do not know anything and (2) we should not feel wise based on our personal filters (1 Corinthians 8:2; Proverbs 3:7).

## Biblical Leader Development

Leader development assesses, challenges, and supports an emerging leader to be more effective. A biblical example of leader development is the relationship between Paul and Timothy. Paul dedicated two books to Timothy to ensure he was directing him toward developing into a godly leader. The scripture that defines Paul's leader development effort is 1 Timothy 4:12–16.

> "Let no one despise you for your youth, but set the believers an example in speech, in conduct, in love, in faith, in purity. Until I come, devote yourself to the public reading of Scripture, to exhortation, to teaching. Do not neglect the gift you have, which was given you by prophecy when the council of elders laid their hands on you. Practice these things; immerse yourself in them, so that all may see your progress. Keep a close watch on

yourself and on the teaching. Persist in this, for by so doing you will save both yourself and your hearers."

Of the three leader development components—assessing, challenging assignments, and supporting a leader to be more effective—Paul focused on giving Timothy a challenging assignment that included establishing a standard of living among his contemporaries, which may be typically uncharacteristic of someone of his age. Paul challenged Timothy behaviorally and intellectually. He also challenged him to persevere, practice discipline, and to become a self-leader.

Although Timothy identified with a younger social group, Paul challenged him to behave like a seasoned believer in the presence of all believers so he could lead by example (1 Timothy 4:12). Leading by example triggers change and causes followers to change their behavioral patterns. Timothy's behavioral standards were to focus on general conversation, love, faith, and purity.

Paul wanted Timothy to be intellectually strong by devoting himself to the reading of the Word, encouraging others in the Word, and teaching the Word (1 Timothy 4:13). The exemplary life of a leader includes doing the cerebral things that jump-started the lifestyle changes that the Scriptures define for all believers.

Paul instructs Timothy to persevere through all challenges, and to continue to practice the behavioral and intellectual tasks assigned to him (1 Timothy 4:14–15). The King James Version uses the word *meditate* instead of the word *practice*, however; the word *meditate* in the Greek lexicon, *meletaō,* means to care for, attend to carefully. This elevates the idea of committing an undefined amount of time to something or someone to ensure its well-being. Here, Paul is teaching Timothy to spend time developing as a leader, display godly behaviors, and build his intellectual capacity.

Lastly, Paul gives Timothy a lesson in self-leadership. Self-leadership is the process of motivating self to achieve personal goals. Paul sets the personal goals for Timothy: "Keep a close watch on yourself and the teaching" (1 Timothy 4:16). The phrase *"keep a close watch"* is defined by the Greek word *epechō,* which means to have or hold upon, apply, to observe, and attend to. The focus Paul is instilling in Timothy is to develop himself, so that he can become the example other believers can rely on, as they continue to grow in the faith. To be an example, Timothy must buy into the idea of self-leadership, which may involve personal development without any reliable support nearby. Self-leadership is not a group effort, but it is an individual effort, of which the framework for self-leadership promotes the tools for behavioral and intellectual change.

**Measuring the Quality of your Leader Development System**

Developing leaders is a challenging and rewarding experience; however, it is important to measure the quality and success of the program along the way so to ensure that the persons that are being developed are receiving the best information possible to reach their leadership potential. There are four metrics that can be used to measure the effectiveness of a leadership development program: (1) alignment with the context of the organization, (2) clear system outcomes, (3) maturing leader competencies, and (4) solution development.

*Alignment with the context of the organization.* The context of an organization refers to the organization's culture. An organization's environment is shaped by variables like organizational structure, organizational systems, leadership structure, and the decision-making process. These variables are important for any leader development program; because they inherently shape the leaders that are being developed. The unique views of an emerging leader's skill set and interests are further framed by environments they are exposed to. Depending on the internal wiring of an emerging leader, the environment that shapes their development can either cause a positive or adverse reaction. This reaction should not be used to define or label an emerging leader. Rather, their reaction should be one of the several tools used to determine if that person is the right fit for the leadership development system. Cutting ties with emerging leaders that do not fit is beneficial for the organization and the emerging leader. It should be noted that every leader developed within the church has a distinct purpose. See what Paul writes in Ephesians 4:11-14. The leaders of the church are formulated for the following purposes:

(1) Equipping the saints for the work of the ministry,

(2) Building up the body of Christ,

(3) Helping saints attain unity of the faith,

(4) Helping saints attain knowledge of the Son of God,

(5) Maturing in the faith, and

(6) No longer confused or persuaded by various doctrines, beliefs, craftiness, and deceit.

This is a tall order, yet it is an accurate depiction of the culture of the church—developing the spiritual life of all believers.

*Clear system outcomes.* What characteristics are important for every leader in your organization to have? Only the organization that is developing leaders can answer this question. As the answer to this question is developed and refined, it must be integrated into the formal leadership development system. At a minimum, all leaders should be capable of influencing others to achieve a common goal. Similarly, all leaders must learn the skill of generating direction, alignment, and commitment among their followers. The intent of developing leaders that are able to produce desired results is to ensure the success of the organization. The church should not view other churches as its competitors; but the church and its many affiliate locations are resource centers for the development of Disciples of Christ. The true competitor of a local church is the *enemy*, who is working over time, to devour as many as he can from the household of faith (1 Peter 5:8-9). The competitive advantage of the church over the enemy has to do with the leaders of the church, as they embody Christ and work in their area of ministry to protect the flock from the enemy's devices.

*Maturing leader competencies.* The expectation people have of their leaders is that they are competent to lead them and capable of integrating the skill sets of the team toward achieving the goals of the team. In most instances, individual team members are focused on their roles and responsibilities and do not concern themselves with the responsibilities of the rest of the team. This is why it is important for the leader to be responsible for providing direction, alignment, and commitment for the team. Otherwise, the team will be at risk of underperforming and losing faith in the leadership capacity of the leader. The Bible tells followers to obey their leaders because they are responsible for watching over their souls (Hebrews 13:17). Although leaders have the right to promote this scripture as a reason to require follower's allegiance, many lose sight of the importance of earning the trust of followers. Aspiring and attaining the title of a leader must be earned. The little secret that is lost in all of this is that: leadership is also sustained by earning the trust of followers.

*Solution development.* The church operates in several business categories; one of which is the solutions business. The ultimate solution that the church provides to its consumer base is salvation through Jesus Christ. In business, the company that develops solutions to meet the needs of their consumers are the companies that earn consumer trust. With this trust, customers return to the same solution provider for answers to new challenges. Within the church, the solution is the same for all challenges—Jesus Christ. Leaders at all levels of the church must be skilled in how they deliver Christ to the persons under their care. Christ alone is offensive to those that live in the dark; but without a good skill, a leader will introduce the right solution the wrong way, and, as a result, lose the opportunity to meet the need of parishioners. Proverbs 11:30

teaches us that the person that wins souls is a wise person.

## Final Thought

Leadership development within the local church is important for the survival of the church. What many pastors do not realize is that their churches are needed in the communities where they operate in. For churches of all sizes to thrive and provide the much needed spiritual support within their communities, pastors must actively engage in leadership development, so that leaders can take their rightful places as ministers that are effective enough to meet the need of souls—both within and outside the four walls of the church.

## Notes

Greek Lexicon: G1907 (KJV). Retrieved from http://www.blueletterbible.orghttps://www.bluelett erbible.org/lang/lexicon/lexicon.cfm

Greek Lexicon: G3191 (KJV). Retrieved from http://www.blueletterbible.orghttps://www.bluelett erbible.org/lang/lexicon/lexicon.cfm

Kantur, D.,&Iseri-Say, A. (2013), Organizational context and firm-level entrepreneurship: a multiple-case analysis.*Journal of Organizational Change Management, 26*(2), 305–325

Neck, C., &Manz, C. (2013). *Mastering self leadership: Empowering yourself for personal excellence.* Upper Saddle River, NJ: Pearson Education.

Northouse, P. (2013). *Leadership: Theory and practice* (6th ed.). Thousand Oaks, CA: Sage.

Schraeder, M., Tears, R., & Jordan, M. (2005). Organizational culture in public sector organizations: Promoting change through training and leading by example. *Leadership & Organization Development Journal, 26*(6), 492–502.

*The English Standard Version Bible*. New York: Oxford University Press, 2009. Print.

Ting, S., & Hart, E. W. (2004). Formal coaching. In C. D. McCauley & E. Van Velsor (Eds.), *The Center for Creative Leadership handbook of leadership development* (2nd ed., pp. 116-150). San Francisco: Jossey-Bass.

Van Velsor, E., McCauley, C. D., &Ruderman, M. N. (2010). The *Center for Creative Leadership handbook of leadership development* (3rd Ed.). San Francisco, CA: Jossey-Bass.

## About the Author

Dr. William Clark is a leadership development specialist and a change management strategist consultant to nonprofits and churches. He has over 10 years experience working in government operations, nonprofit organizations and public housing. Dr. Clark holds a Doctor of Strategic Leadership degree from Regent University and a Masters of Leadership Development degree from Penn State University.

Contact Dr. Clark:

drwilliampclark@gmail.com

www.williampclark.com